The Wind in the Willows Collection

The Flood

Story by Jane Clempner
Illustrated by Andrew Geeson

Based on a Martin Gates Production © 1996 BMG Entertainment,
Licensed by Just Licensing Limited. All rights reserved.
Published in Great Britain in 1997 by World International Ltd.,
Deanway Technology Centre, Wilmslow Road, Handforth, Cheshire SK9 3FB.
Printed in Finland. ISBN 0 7498 2858 7

Spring had arrived on the river bank.

"Might we go for a picnic?" asked Mole, gingerly.

"Splendid idea!" agreed Rat. And they set off at once down the river.

"Just listen," mused Rat.

"I can't hear anything," said Mole.

"Precisely, Moley! Peace-And-Quiet. There's nothing like it!"

B ut before long their peace was shattered by a loud pop-pop-popping noise.

Next moment, Toad careered down the towpath on a motorbike!

"Gangway!" he yelled. "Toad's on the road!" And with that he swerved helplessly down the bank and into the water!

"The River's no place for noisy machines," scolded Rat, hauling Toad from the wreckage.

"Why don't you take up a more leisurely pursuit… like boating?"

"Boating?" scoffed Toad. "Phooey – boating's far too tame for an adventuresome Toad like me!"

The three went back to Rat's snug home on the river bank to dry out.

Some days later, when peace had returned to the river bank, Rat and Mole set out for their picnic once more.

"Any news from Toad?" asked Mole.

"Not a word – too busy with some new fad I shouldn't wonder," tutted Rat.

"Ahoy there, shipmates!" came an excited cry. "Make way for Captain Toad!"

The two friends turned to see a gaily-painted motor launch racing towards them.

A fancy engine at one end and Toad, beaming with pride, at the other!

"How's this for boating?" he called as he sped past, sounding a loud ship's bell and sending ducks a-flying.

Mole clung to the little boat for dear life. "Oh my. Oh my!" he gasped.

Rat was furious. "You water hog!" he shouted. "Have you no respect?"

"It's the life on the waves for me from now on," shouted Toad as he turned to tear back up the river. The startled river-bankers ran for cover.

Which was just as well, for that evening came a terrible storm. The sky grew black and the heavens opened. Lightning ripped across the sky. Rat had never seen such rain.

Luckily Mole had been out walking and found his way safely to Badger's house.

But poor Rat was trapped at home. As the storm raged he barricaded his door against the rising water. But it seeped in through every crack.

Then a mighty wave crashed his door down and the strong current swept all his belongings away!

Meanwhile, Mole paced to and fro.

"Don't fret," urged Badger. "No one knows the river like Ratty."

There was a knock at the door.

"See… that will be him now."

But it was just a small and trembling hedgehog.

"Please, Sir. Come quick," she sobbed. "It's Mister Rat. His home has been swept away!"

Badger and Mole arrived at the river to find Rat holding onto a log wedged in an overhanging willow.

"Don't worry. We'll help you," called Badger.

"My furniture! My beautiful home – it's all gone!" cried Rat.

"Oh my, what can we do?" said Mole.

"Follow me... " ordered Badger, "... to Toad Hall!"

They found Toad taking afternoon tea.

"Ahoy there you fellows," he cried cheerfully. "Bit of a storm in the old teacup!"

"No time for all that," said Badger. "Rat's home has been swept away and we need your assistance."

Toad leapt to his feet. "Just tell me what to do..."

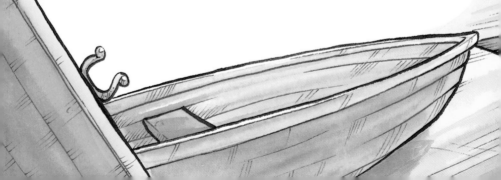

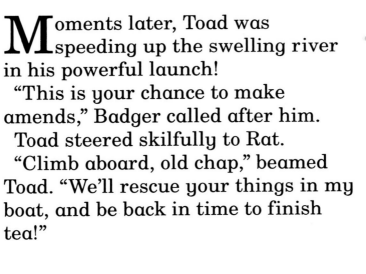

Moments later, Toad was speeding up the swelling river in his powerful launch!

"This is your chance to make amends," Badger called after him.

Toad steered skilfully to Rat.

"Climb aboard, old chap," beamed Toad. "We'll rescue your things in my boat, and be back in time to finish tea!"

Later that spring, when Rat's home was restored and the flood was just a memory, Rat and Mole rowed peacefully into a quiet backwater.

"Third time lucky," smiled Mole, laying out a sumptuous spread. "By the way, what became of Toad's boat?"

"He soon tired of it," sighed Rat. "Otter has turned it upside-down to make a new home!"

Mole lay back on the grassy bank enjoying the warmth of the sun. Suddenly there came a familiar cry. "Look out, chaps. *This* is the way to travel!" Followed by Toad, on a strange-looking bicycle with a sail!

"Oh, Toadie. Will you never learn?" laughed Rat. And the three friends tucked happily into their picnic at last.

The Wind in the Willows Collection©

For you to own on video

Now you can join Mole, Toad, Ratty and Badger on all their adventures in The Wind in the Willows Video Collection.

NEW from September 1996 -
THE ADVENTURES OF TOAD

THE ADVENTURES OF MOLE and
THE ADVENTURES OF TOAD are also
available on story cassettes.

For further information on The Wind in the Willows Collection and BMG's other products, please send your name and address to:

BMG Video
PO Box 607
London SW6 4XR

BMG
V I D E O

Special offer to our Wind In The Willows readers.

every Wind In The Willows book produced by World International Ltd., you
ll find a special token. Collect six tokens and we will send you a super
ng size poster featuring all The Wind In The Willows characters.

eturn this page together with your six tokens to:-

arketing Dept, WITW, World International Ltd, Deanway Technology Centre,
ilmslow Road, Handforth, Cheshire, SK9 3FB

ur Name _____ Age _____

ddress _____

_____

_____

_____ Postcode _____

gnature of Parent/Guardian _____

nclose six tokens - please send me a Wind In The Willows poster.

e may occasionally wish to advise you of other Wind In The Willows gifts. ☐
ou would rather we didn't please tick this box.

Offer open to residents of UK, Channel Isles and Ireland only.

Collect six of these tokens
You will find one inside every
Wind in the Willows book which
has this special offer.

1
TOKEN

Titles in

If you have any difficulty obtaining any of these books, please contact the
Marketing Department at:
World International Limited, Deanway Technology Centre,
Wilmslow Road, Handforth, Cheshire SK9 3FB
Telephone: 01625 650011